Fairy Princess Lolly

Herb Leonhard

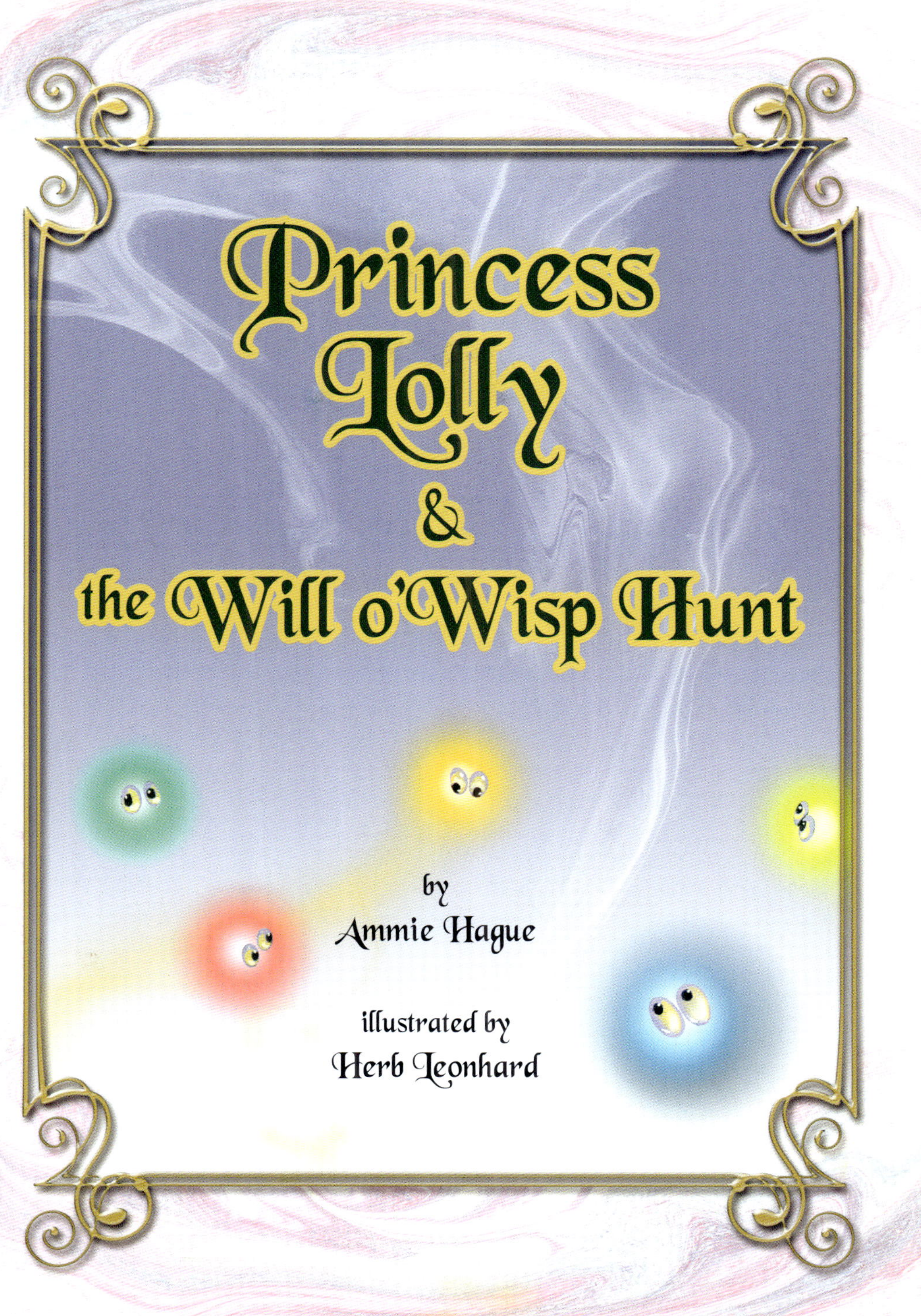
Princess Lolly
&
the Will o'Wisp Hunt

by
Ammie Hague

illustrated by
Herb Leonhard

Dedication

It is of course appropriate to have a well-polished list of highly-deserving individuals upon whom I shall heap my gratitude but every time I vigorously rub the page it just makes a mess!

Thus I would like to dedicate this, my first book, to my mom, dad and brothers (Patricia Shaw, Don Hague, Ryan Hague and Brandon Fielding) who have been ever supportive and just as crazy as any other family in the world.
Also, my three fury felines, Wotan the Faerie Smasher and last but not least…

…every muse that inspires, and dreamer that reaches for the golden ring…

I kaimel coa: The Dream Lives!

c.p. *Fatima Kilrain ní Fiona*

Text © 2014 by Ammie Hague
Illustrations © 2014 by Herb Leonhard
Wotan the Faerie Smasher appears courtesy of and © 2014 Eric Pope

www.guildedquill.net
www.herbleonhard.com

ISBN number: 978-0-9763555-7-1
Library of Congress Control Number: 2013923571

Published in the United States of America by The Prancing Pony.
Printed in Hong Kong.

There once was a bright Fairy Princess
Whose title was nigh ostentatious
To avoid royal folly
They just called her Lolly
And went on about their business

When her lessons were done each day,
Princess Lolly whiled hours away
Making mischief and mayhem
All over the Kingdom
(More fun than being Queen, I daresay)

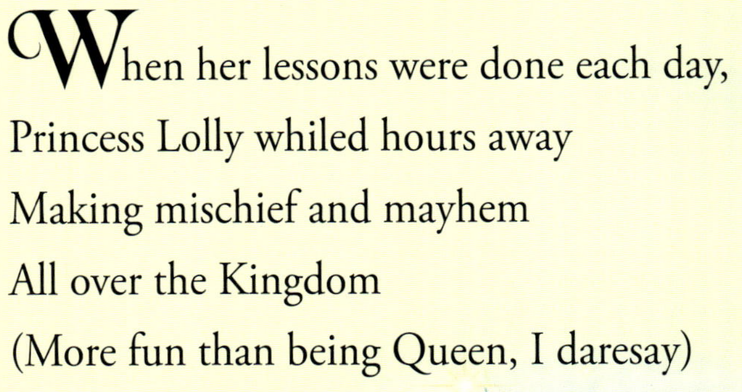

Shenanigans were her favorite thing
Giant croquet and barbarian baiting
But on this particular eve
The Princess set out with great speed
To go wild will o' the wisp hunting!

As she prepared to exeunt the castle
She thought, "It sure would be razzle-dazzle,
"To bring my magical friends
"Connor, and Tristan the Dragon."
And invited them along without hassle

Now the trio of friends started talking
Whilst into Sherwood Forest were walking
When they were joined by Lili
A silly, young Ghillie
Who told them no wisps were a' frolickling

No glowing orbs? Well, that was bunk!
Into the woods the four friends slunk
Tiptoeing down the path
They so happened to pass
A will o' wisp stuck in a tree trunk!

"How now, Will o'Wisp, what is this?"
"I'm stuck in this stump fair Princess!"
So Lili climbed the tree,
And plucked the bauble free
Quite grateful, the Wisp whispered this:

"Other wisps are hidden around.
Some in the woods or in town.
We got lost on our romp
Venturing out from the swamp.
Please help get us back to our grounds!"

So the quadruplet set off in a jiffy
Headed past the local blacksmithy
They espied a warm light,
Glowing like coals in the night
Whom Tristan the Dragon freed quickly

The intrepid bunch searched low and high
Wedged in some stones heard a will o'wisp cry
Connor moved all the rocks
He was as strong as an ox!
And the wisp floated up in the sky

By the joust field they paused for a rest
And chatted about games they liked best
Where Lolly saw on the quintain
A wisp struggling in vain
Whom she rescued without any protest

Where should they look next? They pondered
As the four friends idly wandered
For a very long spell
Over hill, across dale
Under bushes? In holes? Over yonder?

But the next will o'wisp posed a surprise
For right before the fairy troop's eyes
Tangled up in the branches
A sphere struggled hapless
A plan of action they had to devise!

The gang rallied together to confer
Deciding that this required teamwork
To relieve the orb's distress
A toadstool pile would be best
To stack up and use as a ladder

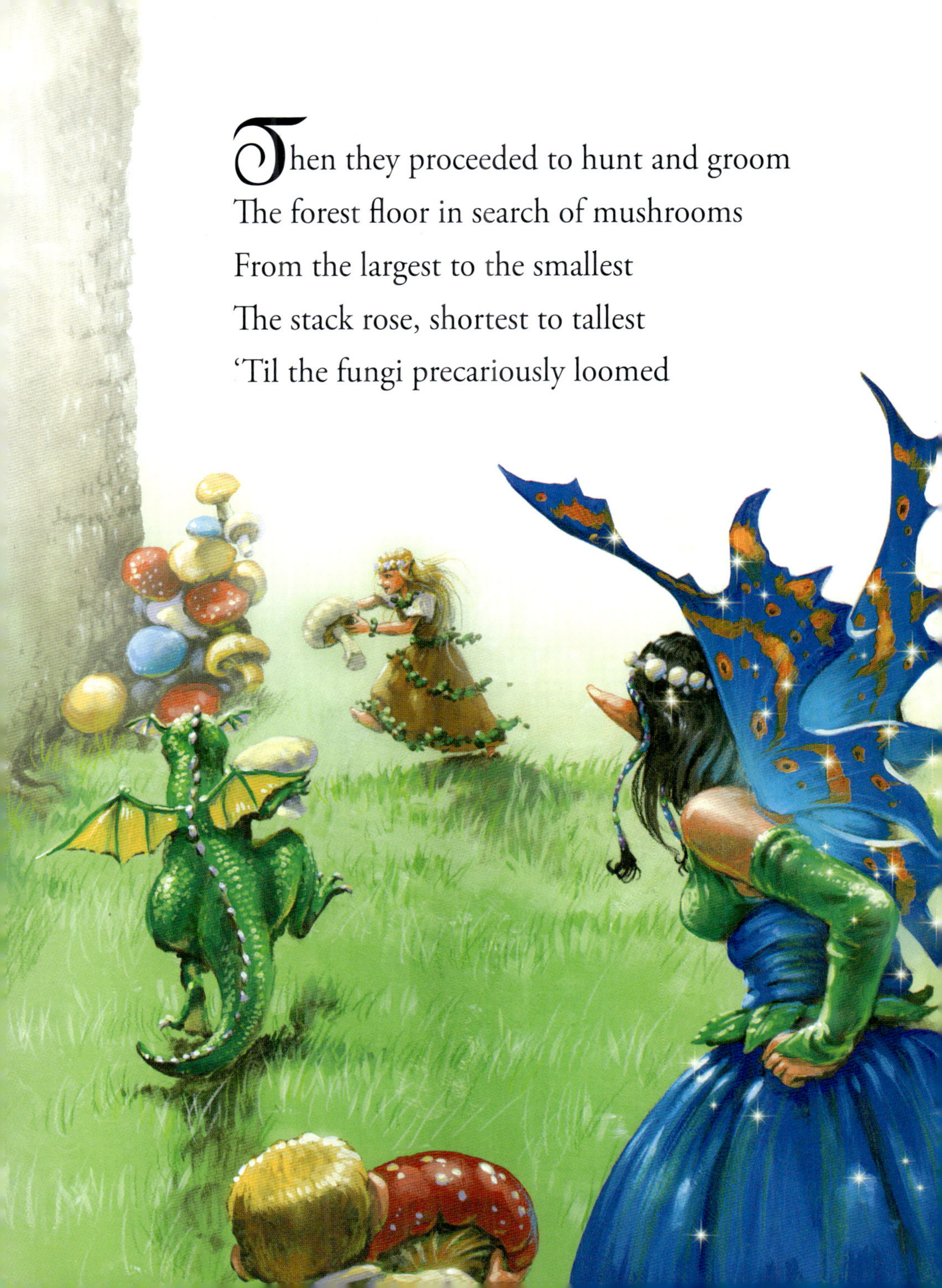

Then they proceeded to hunt and groom

The forest floor in search of mushrooms

From the largest to the smallest

The stack rose, shortest to tallest

'Til the fungi precariously loomed

Princess Lolly directed the production
Using strength, Connor held the foundation
Lili waited with a net
While Tristan climbed the turret
And she caught the wisp, soft as a cushion

Cheers of "Huzzah!" and "Hurrah!" filled the air
For the crew was all the more merrier
They had planned to success
And found the will o'wisps
Gathering them all up with due care

Throughout Sherwood Forest they roamed
Returning the Wisps to their home
When one whispered to Lolly,
"It'd be great if ye'd follow me,
I think my friend's lost in the gloam."

Instead of going along splendid
It suddenly all was upended
Because wisps by their natures
Just love to be pranksters
So the Princess they kind of misled

Although Her Highness was dubious
She followed because she was curious
With a splash through the bog
She got lost in the fog
The whole situation was spurious!

When the mists finally cleared for the damsel
She said, "This detour home leaves me frazzled.
I'm in a place called Wenatchee
Where ever that might be
And must be getting back to my castle!"

So that's where this fairytale ends
Worry not! For another begins
Princess Lolly is clever
And won't stay lost forever
She'll again reunite
with her friends!

to be continued...

Cast of Characters:

Tristan Sajovic

is a kindergartner from Oregon who began his rise to stardom upon the flying trapeze! He is an accomplished trampoline jumper. At Renaissance Faires he transforms to become Tristan the Dragon, a familiar of the Mongers Guild, a group of blacksmithing educators and demonstrators. He also makes and sells felted dragon eggs.

Liliana Gnos

is a third-grader from Oregon with a penchant for splashing in streams, running around barefoot and wearing flowers in her hair. She makes and sells hand-made soap (which probably helps with cleaning dirty feet). Also a member of the Mongers Guild, Liliana is studying fiber arts such as spinning and weaving. Some of her favorite hobbies include reading and ballet.

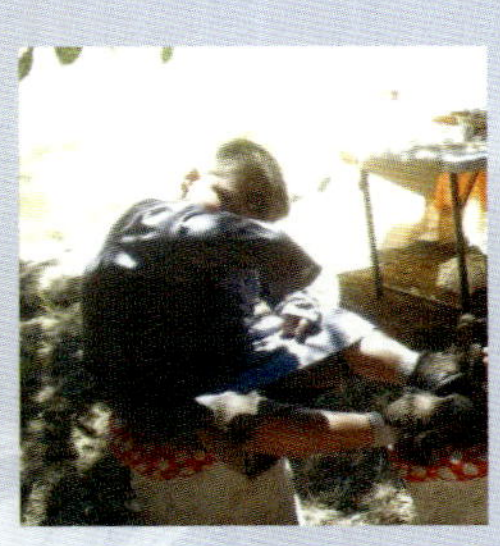

Connor

is a gregarious first-grader whose favorite color is purple. Being quite strong for his size, he is an excellent helper and protector of other children. Although Connor has had training in the ways of becoming a squire, we Faeries know that he secretly wields magical powers and that he knows how to use a wand.

Fairy Princess Lolly

Her Royal Highness Fairy Princess Fatima Tempest Kilrain ni Fiona (told you it was ostentatious!) was born at Castle Dragonsong within the Kingdom of Storms.

She notoriously loves candy (but not chocolate), fabulously bright colors and has a secret treasury filled with dross given to her by children. Princess Lolly can be found where the veil between worlds blurs: Renaissance Faires, Conventions, Festivals bringing to life these very stories with children of all ages, shapes and sizes.

You can find her on the Book of Faces at: **facebook.com/LollysCastle**

Herb Leonhard

Herb Leonhard was born in Munich, Germany but grew up in the United States. One of his earliest memories was of a series of German children's books beautifully illustrated by Fritz Baumgarten. This, along with a childhood spent within the pages of comics, inevitably led to a career as an artist with a love of classic illustration.

With more than 30 books to his credit, he remains able to observe the natural world around us with a sense of wonder, and sees every subsequent painting and drawing as a new learning experience.

He lives in the American Pacific Northwest with his wife, son, two horses, four cats and a plethora of chickens.

His work can be seen at: **www.herbleonhard.com**

Contributors

We would like to sincerely thank all of the magical people that contributed to our Kickstarter to bring these stories to life.

Jim "I Do Believe in Fairies" Swain
Philip Eventide
Mean Kitty Wear
Chloe
Doug Spaulding
Lisa Robinson
Doug & Joy Staudt
Insatia
Doctora Reina
Alisa Anguiano
Crescent Moon Gifts
RadCon
Shrewsbury Renaissance Faire
Brenda the Royal Hair Braider
   brendathebraider.com
Brian Rowe
Megan Cowan
Teddy Harman
Joe O'Rear
Todd Branch
E.Luminarius Brightwick
David McFarland
Trek
Duchess Lelie, Regent of Willows
Terry Fish
William J. (B.J.) Altman
Bryan Sapphire, The Evil Juggler
Jamie, Natalya and Tristan Sajovic
Tanaria
Brian Kowalczyk
Liliyana
Joshua Books
Micheal "The Viking" Gustafson
Annie
Summer Dawn Campbell
Marier Family
Matthew and Jennifer York
The Fool
jennyusagi
Kasandra Gillum
Tony Davis
Jason Andrew
Jason
Nora Timmerman

Patricia Shaw
Jonnalyhn Wolfcat
Sigmata
Mahlora
Aaron Alberg
Robin Family
Olivia and Elizabeth Davis
Chris Schetzle
Kelly and Julia Pohl
Elspeth Götz
Scott & Andrea Sutherlin
Kammie & Emmie Edwards
Michael Hanscom
Lady La De Dah
Chuck Childers
Michael J. Pucci
Raymond Macalino
Andrew Harris
Matthew Sanderson
Christopher Sanders
Betsy Sauther
aquariann.com
Eschaton Media
Amy Brown
Ted Gill
Joanne Percy
The Fairies Coomes
Her Majesty, Queen Ilex Aquifolia
   of the Maryland Faerie Festival
Victoria Lane
Chloe Emerson
Dennis Carr
Pottery Crone Cindy Nielsen
Linda M. Crate
Shane Scott Freund
Jeff Isaak
Frostey Knight
Brianna Firefly
Mark C
Leaf McGowan
Sophia, Dario, Alvina, Poppy
   & Sailor
Ken Reinertson
Arron Mitchell
Raven, Anastasia, & Caelan

Dylan Birtolo
Jennifer Baker
Eldenath S. de Vilya
Fred Zeleny
MoJo
Randy, Char, Iaine & Aydan
   Mac Kay
Baroness Dorian Gayle
Susan Schroder
Sienna R. Williams
Ed "Angus" Matuskey
Nick Plantz
Jane Van Kleeck
Tim and Cheryl Martin
Lindsey Morse
The Convy's
Lori K Fisher
Tarah Wheeler Van Vlack
Jen Page
VooDoo
Julzerator
Vicki Welch
Sir Darian Strongstar
The Lees
Lauren Ellis
Jason Walter
April R. Robinson
Amber DiSimone
Libby Cook
Galen Ciscell
Shelly Honeysuckle
The Wandering Lou
Charlie Perez
Erik Bridge
Michael Shaudis
Don Hague
Patricia Shaw
Ye Merrie Greenwood Players
Susan Adams
Chateau Boudreaux
Erin R. Hogan
Shelley Davis
SpoCon
Posh Rat Productions